BUILDING
WORLD LANDMARKS

The Louvre

by Sudipta Bardhan-Quallen

BLACKBIRCH PRESS
An imprint of Thomson Gale, a part of The Thomson Corporation

THOMSON
GALE

Detroit • New York • San Francisco • San Diego • New Haven, Conn. • Waterville, Maine • London • Munich

PICTURE CREDITS: Cover image: © Gabriela Medina/SuperStock
AFP/Getty Images, 39
© Bettmann/CORBIS, 5
© Corel Corporation, 24
© Dave G. Houser, 32
Erich Lessing/Art Resource, NY, 9, 19
Giraudon/Art Resource, NY, 29
Giraudon/Bridgeman Art Library, 12 (bottom)
Hulton/Archive by Getty Images, 12 (top), 37
Mary Evans Picture Library, 22
Musee de la Ville de Paris, Musee Carnavalet, Paris, France, J.P. Zenobel/Bridgeman Art Library, 16
Private Collection, The Stapleton Collection/Bridgeman Art Library, 14-15
Richard I'anson/Lonely Planet Images, 42
Scala/Art Resource, NY, 30
Suzanne Santillan, 34

LIBRARY OF CONGRESS CATALOGING-IN-PUBLICATION DATA

Bardhan-Quallen, Sudipta.
   The Louvre / by Sudipta Bardhan-Quallen.
     p. cm. — (Building world landmarks)
   Includes bibliographical references and index.
   ISBN 1-4103-0567-8
     1. Louvre (Paris, France)—History. 2. Paris (France)—Buildings, structures, etc. 3. France—Kings and rulers—Dwellings. 4. Musée du Louvre—History. 5. Museums—France—Paris—History. I. Title. II. Series.
   DC782.L6B28 2005
   727',7'0944361—dc22

                        2005010451

Table of Contents

Centuries in the Making

THE LOUVRE IN Paris, France, is one of the most famous buildings in the world. It has been a military fortress, a royal residence, an artists' commune, and an administrative building. As an art museum, it attracts almost 6 million visitors a year. From an architectural standpoint, the Louvre is much more than a building. Writer and photographer Nicolas d'Archimbaud notes, "The Louvre is a book of stone in which eight centuries of French architecture have been chronicled."[1]

Over the centuries, the Louvre has been transformed repeatedly. As additions were made to the Louvre, different architectural styles were introduced. Sometimes, older structures were demolished to make room for new constructions. More often than not, new wings were merely added on to the older building, and architects made an effort to balance, rather than match, the older styles.

In recent years, another extensive renovation of the Louvre has taken place. The Grand Louvre Project, begun by French president François Mitterrand, successfully updated the Louvre to bring it into the twenty-first century while preserving its historic beauty. Genevieve Bresc-Bautier, chief curator of the Department of Sculpture at the Louvre, writes: "The Louvre is sometimes called the greatest and largest museum in the world, but that is only one aspect of it. It is itself rich in history, and it brings together the wealth of a nation for display to all who choose to come. . . . Centuries old but ever new, the palace distils and transmits the consciousness of art."[2]

Begun in 1190 as a military fortress, the Louvre in Paris is today one of the most impressive buildings in the world.

A Royal Heritage

THE LOUVRE'S STORY began in 1190, when King Philippe Auguste of France built a fortress on the banks of the Seine River. Situated on a site called the Louvre, the moated castle was built to defend the western boundary of Paris against possible attacks. The four outer walls formed a rough square, with the east and west walls measuring 235 feet (71.6m) long and the north and south walls measuring 255 feet (77.7m) long. Within the castle walls stood a circular keep, or tower, which housed the royal treasury, the king's archives, and even prisoners. The Louvre's keep was called the Great Tower because it was 100 feet (30.5m) tall and 50 feet (15.25m) in diameter—about two-thirds of the height of the Statue of Liberty in New York.

Early Transformations

Over time, the Louvre was transformed. By the reign of Charles V in the fourteenth century, it had become a royal palace. Charles's architect, Raymond du Temple, renovated the original square structure. Along the north and east outer walls, he created a chapel and separate chambers for the king and queen, and laid out gardens to the north and south.

After du Temple's renovations, the Louvre was considered a fairy-tale castle. Author Alexandra Bonfante-Warren describes the building as "a snow-white confection iced with shimmering ceramic tiles, spiky with graceful round turrets."[3] By 1528, however, the fairy-tale castle had been abandoned for more than 150 years. It was in a state of disrepair when François I, who wanted a proper palace in Paris, decided to change the Louvre again.

A Proper Palace

In February 1528, François decided to demolish the Great Tower. The ground where it once stood was paved to create a courtyard. In 1546, François appointed painter and architect Pierre Lescot to design the new palace. Jean Goujon, a noted sculptor, was asked to help with the design.

Lescot designed new facades (the decorative outer layers of walls) for the west and south sides of the Louvre. Above the doors on the ground floor were large circular windows called oculi. The two lower floors had columns at regular intervals. Between the columns were arched windows on the ground floor and large rectangular windows on the second floor. On the third floor, the windows were flanked by figures carved by Goujon. Goujon also created reliefs, or

The Salle des Caryatides

When François I decided to transform the Louvre into a grand palace, he was intent on building a magnificent reception hall. He did not live long enough to see this reception hall completed. However, his son, Henri II, commissioned architects Pierre Lescot and Jean Goujon to create the Salle des Caryatides (Caryatid Room) to fulfill François I's wishes. The room was built in 1550.

A caryatid is a carved standing female figure used in place of a column. Goujon carved four 13-foot-tall (4m) caryatids to uphold the musicians' gallery at one end of the room. On the opposite side was the royal box where the king would stand.

From the beginning, Goujon's caryatid sculptures were admired by all. As author Nicholas d'Archimbaud writes in *Louvre: Portrait of a Museum*, "These figures have lost none of their youthful bloom. Their fluid forms seem susceptible only to the currents and breezes of water and air." Today, the Salle des Caryatides holds the Louvre's collection of Greek sculpture, though visitors come to admire Goujon's work and the room itself as much as the artworks on display.

Four carved female figures known as caryatids support the musicians' gallery in the Salle des Caryatides.

decorative scenes carved onto flat stone surfaces, above the windows on the second floor.

One feature of the facades that was new to France was polychromy, the use of different materials to create a multicolored effect. The facades were mainly made of cream-colored limestone. Over the limestone, the architects applied a fine-grained white stone that was carved into decorative forms. Marble of different colors was also used to form plaques and symbols on the facades.

Additions to the Louvre

In 1556, Lescot added the Pavilion du Roi (King's Pavilion) to the Louvre. It was built in the southwest corner of the original square structure and became the king's official residence until late in the seventeenth century. To decorate the facade of the Pavilion du Roi, Lescot lined the vertical sides with blocks, called quoins, which alternated between long and short. The quoins were decorated by vermiculated rustication, a pattern carved into the stone to look like worms had burrowed into the surface. This type of decoration had never before been used in France.

In 1566, Lescot began to build a new wing, the Petite Galerie, which extended out from the square structure of the original Louvre. On one end of the Petite Galerie was the Pavilion du Roi; on the other end was the Seine River. At this same time, Catherine de Medici, mother of the current king Charles IX, began to build a palace called the Tuileries on a site a short distance from the Louvre. Both the Tuileries and the Petite Galerie remained unfinished during Charles's reign.

The Bourbons' Grand Design

After Charles, very little work was accomplished on the Louvre until 1594, when Henri de Bourbon became Henri IV, king of France. Henri decided to make the Louvre his primary residence in Paris. In fact, according to Bresc-Bautier, Henri wanted to make the Louvre "into a great symbolic palace, in the capital, at the heart of the kingdom, where the various branches of power would be brought together with the royal collections behind walls whose decorative symbolism . . . would proclaim the monarchy."[4]

Henri's plan, called the Grand Dessein (Grand Design), was to link the Louvre and the Tuileries on both sides with two long wings and a system of courtyards. The first of these long wings, which ran along the Seine and was called the Grande Galerie, was designed in 1595 by architects Louis Métézeau and Jacques Androuet du Cerceau.

It took eleven years to complete the Grande Galerie. It measured 1640 feet (500m) long and more than 100 feet (30.5m) wide—longer than four football fields and wider than a baseball diamond. At the time, it was the longest building of its kind in the world. However, Henri did not live to see the rest of his Grand Dessein completed. After he was assassinated in 1610, all work on the Louvre ceased for many years.

The Colonnade

Work on the Louvre began again in 1660, when Henri IV's grandson, Louis XIV, was king. Louis first

*Above, the Louvre
as it looked in
1625. At right, the
interior of the
Grande Galerie as
it looks today.*

completed earlier projects, such as the facade of the Grande Galerie, which had been left unfinished since the time of Henri IV. Louis' main interest, however, was in enhancing the east wing of the Louvre, where he planned to place the new royal apartments. As Bresc-Bautier writes, "This range . . . was to be given a dramatic facade that would express the power of the King and proclaim the notions of royal glory and grandeur which the court was concerned to cultivate."[5] For this wing, Louis turned to Gian Lorenzo Bernini, a favorite architect of the pope.

Bernini was famous for designing the colonnade (a row of columns joined at their tops by a roof) of Saint Peter's Basilica in Rome. Louis desired such a colonnade for the east wing of the Louvre. Bernini sketched out four designs for the colonnade before he was invited to France by the king. He was honored by Louis upon his arrival, and on June 17, 1665, a ceremony was held to begin construction of Bernini's final design. Louis himself laid the first stone of the new facade. Three days later, Bernini returned to Italy, but his vision was never realized. Though Louis may have been excited about an Italian architect working on a French landmark, other French architects were not as enthusiastic. Bernini's plans were shelved.

Instead, in May 1666, a plan set forth by French architects Louis Le Vau, Claude Perrault, and Charles LeBrun was approved by Louis. They designed a 600-foot (183m) facade for the existing east wing that had three stories. The first floor was plain with evenly

In this seventeenth-century engraving, construction is underway on the Colonnade at the palace's main entrance.

spaced window openings. The second floor was decorated with a series of twenty-eight paired columns. The column pairs were also evenly spaced but placed between the window openings of the first floor. A triangular structure called a pediment spanned the tops of the middle eight columns. It would be carved with a decorative scene.

For just over a decade, from 1667 to 1678, work on the Colonnade continued as planned. The project, however, was mostly abandoned in 1678 when Louis XIV shifted his court—and his attention—to the Versailles palace. The exterior of the Colonnade was left

unfinished—most of the stones were left rough, waiting to be sculpted.

Life After the King

When the king moved out, the Louvre became home to the royal administration, academics, and artists. The building's time as a royal residence had come to an end. For more than seventy years, no real improvements were made to the Louvre. When things did change, the goal was no longer to transform the Louvre into a palace fit for a king—rather, people began to envision a grand museum.

An Idea for a Museum

YEARS OF NEGLECT took its toll on the Louvre. The entire structure fell into disrepair. For example, when the Colonnade was built, the columns held up lintels (horizontal beams of stones that ran across the top of the columns). By 1753, the iron rods that had been used to hold the enormous lintels together had rusted and split the stones around them. This damage had to be repaired immediately to save the facade from collapse. Renovations quickly began on various parts of the building.

In the course of the renovations, the idea of transforming the building into a museum came about. In Rome, the pope's art collection was already available for the public to see—people in France felt the French royal collections should also be on display. French politician Jean-Marie Roland imagined a museum that would "nourish a taste for the fine arts, create new art

In 1764, workers clear debris from the Louvre's Colonnade after years of neglect caused the palace to fall into disrepair.

lovers, and serve as a school for artists; it must be open to all. The monument must be a national one."[6]

A Revolutionary Idea

During the French Revolution of 1789, the monarchy was removed from power. In its place, a democratic government was established. The French people felt that pleasures such as art should no longer be reserved for royalty and nobility. The Louvre was converted into a public art museum, the Musée Central de la République, which opened on August 10, 1793.

In the years following the revolution, work continued on the Louvre. Most of this work, however, was minor and had more to do with repairing damage than adding to the building. The outlook for the Louvre began to change in 1799, when Napoléon Bonaparte, a French general, was named head of the French government.

Napoléon's Support

Napoléon was a great supporter of the Louvre as an art museum. In 1803, the museum was renamed the Musée Napoléon to honor its patron. When Napoléon crowned himself emperor in 1804, he viewed the Louvre as a symbol of his power, just as the kings before him had. In the eleven years that Napoléon ruled France, notes d'Archimbaud, "the Louvre grew in size and glory to become a center of European art."[7] Napoléon revived the Grand Dessein and aimed to complete the task of linking the Louvre to the Tuileries.

Napoléon appointed architects Pierre Fontaine and Charles Percier to finish the Grand Dessein. The architects wanted to demolish parts of the older building to create a more unified effect, but Napoléon felt strongly that the Louvre's history should be preserved. He said, "The architects wish to adopt a single order and change everything. Economy, common sense and good taste are opposed to this; we should leave to each of the parts that exist the character of its own age."[8] Therefore, the vast majority of the original Louvre was preserved under Napoléon.

Despite his efforts, Napoléon did not complete the Grand Dessein. He built a road, the Rue de Rivoli, to make room for the new wing that would link the Louvre and the Tuileries on the opposite side of the Grande Galerie. He even drove out all the artists, administrators, and courtiers who had rooms at the

Pope Pius VII and other church officials watch as Napoléon crowns himself emperor of France in 1804.

Louvre to facilitate the construction, but no meaningful work was begun before Napoléon was exiled.

Afterward Napoléon was forced into exile in 1815. France went through a great deal of political turmoil. The Louvre remained a symbol of power, and so every government after Napoléon established itself in the Louvre. The next major addition to the Louvre, however, did not take place until Louis-Napoléon Bonaparte, the nephew of Napoléon I and better known as Napoléon III, came to power.

The Grand Design Is Completed

In 1848, the French government decided to complete the Grand Dessein. There was no immediate plan, however, on how to proceed, and the government did not have the funds to complete the project. After Bonaparte was elected president of France in December 1848, general repairs of the Grande Galerie and Petite Galerie began, including the completion of the carvings on the pediments of these wings.

In December 1851, Bonaparte named himself Emperor Napoléon III. He followed in his uncle's footsteps and made great additions to the Louvre. Finally, centuries after the Grand Dessein was conceived, Napoléon III completed it.

In 1852, Napoléon III appointed an architect, Louis-Tullius-Joachim Visconti, to design the final wing of the Louvre complex. This wing would be named in honor of Cardinal Richelieu, the chief minister of Louis XIII, who had acquired great works of art for the monarchy. Visconti completed a design, but died before any work

The Arc de Triomphe du Carrousel

Napoléon I intended to finish the Grand Dessein, but never accomplished it. Still, he made great additions to the Louvre, especially to the exterior decorations. One prominent example was the Arc de Triomphe du Carrousel, a structure that measured 63 feet (19.2m) high, 75 feet (22.3m) wide, and 24 feet (7.3m) deep and that cost more than 1.4 million francs to build. It was built between 1806 and 1808, early in Napoléon's reign. This stone arch monument with detailed carvings was raised to honor Napoléon's Grande Armée, which had achieved so much military success for France. The carvings depicted Napoléon's treaties and military campaigns. The arch acted as the ceremonial entrance to the courtyard of the Tuileries.

Napoléon appointed the best sculptors and painters of the age to work on the monument. The structure is made of three arches: a large central arch, 21 feet (6.4m) high and 9 feet (2.7m) wide, surrounded by two smaller arches, more than 14 feet (4.3m) high and 9 feet (2.7m) wide. The front of the arch is decorated with eight columns made of red marble. These columns were found in the Louvre's storage, along with other building materials abandoned since the reign of Louis XIV. Crowning each of the columns is the statue of a soldier of the Grande Armée: a dragoon, an infantry grenadier, an armored cavalry, a cavalry chasseur, a grenadier, a gunner, a rifleman, and a sapper.

was done. Architect Hector-Martin Lefuel took Visconti's place and headed up a team of 3,000 workmen. Construction began on August 14, 1857.

The first step toward building the new wing was to demolish all the public houses that stood between the two palaces. Many people were evicted from their homes. Next, the north wing was built along the Rue de Rivoli. This addition created a courtyard between

This nineteenth-century illustration shows the completed Louvre, with the Cour Napoléon standing between the palace's wings.

the new wing, the Grande Galerie, and the west wing of the original Louvre. This courtyard was named the Cour Napoléon in honor of Napoléon III.

Lefuel added a large number of sizeable statues to the facades of the Louvre. On the facades facing the Cour Napoléon, Lefuel mounted 83 statues of famous and influential French men. These statues were 10 feet (3.1m) tall and stood on the terraces of the second floor of the building. On the facade facing the Rue de Rivoli, Lefuel placed 8 statues of leaders of Napoléon I's armies. Lefuel also added statues of seated figures or 6-foot-tall (1.8m) putti (babies) along the roofline of the building. The putti represented the seasons, continents, arts, trades, and sciences.

In total, the project of finishing Henri IV's plan took over a decade and required more than 500 workers to toil by day and, with the invention of early electric lights called arc lights, by night. The completed Grand Dessein created a massive Louvre complex—the courtyards enclosed by the various wings were roughly the size of four and a half football fields placed side by side.

When the Grand Dessein was completed, Napoléon III decribed it as "the realization of a grand design instinctively approved by the nation for more than a hundred years."[9] The Grand Dessein did not make a very lasting impression, though, as the Tuileries was burned down just a few years after the work was completed. On May 23, 1871, during a civil war, forces opposing the government set fire to the Tuileries and the library of the Louvre. The museum was saved, but the Tuileries was destroyed.

In 1882, the remains of the Tuileries were finally demolished. The loss of the Tuileries signaled a change in the history of the Louvre. No longer a seat of government power, the Louvre became almost exclusively devoted to the arts.

A World-Class Collection

FROM THE BEGINNING of its time as a museum, the Louvre's art collection was quite extensive, since a large part of it was once the royal collection of the king of France. Throughout history, kings were great patrons of the arts, as they were among the few people who could afford to pay for something that served no other purpose than to be beautiful.

The Beginning of the Royal Collection

The French royal art collection, which would become the Louvre's collection, essentially began with François I. Before François, French palaces were poorly decorated. There was a small number of paintings and no sculpture. François began to acquire major artworks either by commissioning them or buying existing works.

The Mona Lisa *is Leonardo Da Vinci's most famous painting and the Louvre's most celebrated piece.*

François acquired paintings by artists such as Raphael, who had painted frescoes in the Vatican, and Michelangelo, who had painted the ceiling of the Sistine Chapel. In addition, François invited prominent artists to come to the French court—among them, an Italian artist named Leonardo da Vinci. Da Vinci came to France in 1516 and was given the titles "first painter" and "engineer and architect of the king."

The Most Famous Painting

While at the French court, da Vinci continued to paint, producing masterpieces such as *The Virgin of the Rocks* and *Saint Anne and the Virgin*. Da Vinci's greatest work, however, came with him from Italy. It was a little-known painting called *La Gioconda* in Italian and known in English as the *Mona Lisa.*

François thought enough of the *Mona Lisa* to buy it after da Vinci's death. The king hung the painting in a prominent place in the royal palace at Fontainebleau, where visitors from all over Europe admired it. The artistic world, however, did not take great notice of the painting until much later.

The *Mona Lisa* did not come to the Louvre until after the French Revolution. Sometime in the middle of the nineteenth century, artists rediscovered the painting and began to study it. The *Mona Lisa's* fame increased when it was stolen from the Louvre in 1911 and returned two years later. Over time, it became arguably the most famous painting in the world.

Napoléon's Additions

Da Vinci may have been the best-known artist at François's court, but he was by no means the only one there. François also invited artists such as Andrea del Sarto, Titian, and Primaticcio, all of whom left their mark on Renaissance art. After François's death in 1547, French kings continued the tradition of building the royal art collection. By the end of Louis XIV's reign, in 1715 there were almost 1,500 major paintings in the collection.

By the time the French monarchy was overthrown and Napoléon Bonaparte became emperor, the Louvre had been transformed into an art museum. The royal collection had become the state's collection. Napoléon carried on the tradition of collecting art—when he went on military campaigns, he brought along experts whose job was to pick through the artwork in conquered territories. These experts would decide which pieces of art would be sent back to France to be displayed at the Louvre. In this way, Napoléon created the best art collection in the world.

Egyptian Antiquities

In 1798, Napoléon brought an expert named Baron Dominique-Vivant Denon on a campaign to Egypt. During this trip, Denon discovered ancient Egyptian artifacts. He sent crates full of mummies, statuettes, and other pieces back to the Louvre.

Denon's interest in Egyptian artifacts led to the formation of the Louvre's Department of Egyptian Antiquities in 1826. Egyptologist Jean-François

Champollion, who had discovered how to decode hieroglyphs, was appointed curator. He was responsible for building the collection by purchasing Egyptian collections from individuals and by sponsoring excavations in Egypt. The Louvre's collection grew extensively until 1922, when the Egyptian government decided to keep most Egyptian artifacts inside the country.

Among the treasures that are found in the Louvre are the Mastaba, or tomb, of Akhethotep, which was transported to the Louvre in pieces packed in 50 crates, and the *Great Sphinx*. The sphinx has the head of a pharaoh, or king, of Egypt with his ceremonial headdress and the body of a lion. This 4,000- to 5,000-year-old sculpture is made of red granite and is 81 inches (205.7cm) high and 136 inches (345.4cm) long.

Replacements Needed

Indirectly, Napoléon's Egyptian campaign led to the Louvre's collection of Egyptian antiquities. Even after Napoléon was sent into exile, interest in these artifacts continued to grow. In this way, Napoléon's influence had a long-lasting positive effect on the Louvre.

In other ways, however, Napoléon's influence did not last as long. Many of the artistic treasures he brought back from conquered territories were returned to their original owners after Napoléon was ousted from power. In 1815, the Louvre's collection lost more than 5,000 pieces of art.

The Louvre's director, Count de Forbin, began to search for other pieces to replace the lost artwork. Forbin particularly wanted to acquire a classical Greek statue. In 1815, the *Apollo Belvedere*, which, had been the Louvre's most admired classical statue, was returned to the Vatican. In addition, just a few months later, in 1816, the British Museum acquired a number of classical sculptures from the Parthenon building in Greece. Since both Italy and England had classical masterpieces, Forbin felt France needed one as well.

In 1815, the Louvre returned Apollo Belvedere, a classical Greek statue, to the Vatican in Rome.

A Statue from Melos

On April 8, 1820, a statue was uncovered on the island of Melos, off the coast of Greece. At the time, French and Greek authorities were convinced that the statue, called the *Venus de Milo* (Venus of Melos), was carved during the classical age in Greece, sometime between the fifth and fourth centuries B.C. For 1,000 francs, French officials on Melos purchased the statue and sent it to the Louvre.

When the *Venus de Milo* arrived, it came with another bundle containing sever al pieces of marble found near the statue. One of the pieces was a base that fit perfectly against the left side of the statue. An inscription on the base read: "Alexandros, son of Menides, citizen of Antioch of Meander made the statue."

Unfortunately for Forbin, who had desperately wanted a classical Greek statue, Antioch was a Greek city that had not been founded until the late third century B.C., 500 years after Greece's classical age ended. The *Venus de Milo* was therefore Hellenistic, not classical. Forbin, however, did not let the inconvenience of the base interfere with his museum's new masterpiece. He decided that there was no definite proof that the base belonged with the statue, so it was not necessary to display the base at all.

Forbin's maneuver may have worked, except that a few scholars had seen the base and inscription before it was removed from view. They published a pamphlet about the Hellenistic origins of the *Venus de Milo* using a sketch of the statue and base made by an art student who had seen both pieces together.

The Venus de Milo, *housed in the Louvre, is the best known sculpture in the world.*

For the next 130 years, French authorities insisted that the *Venus de Milo* was classical, whereas many other scholars claimed that the statue was Hellenistic. The controversy helped to create interest in the statue, and visitors crowded to the Louvre to see what was causing all the fuss.

By 1951, when the French admitted that the *Venus de Milo* was likely not a classical statue, its fame was well established. In fact, according to journalist Gregory Curtis, "The *Venus de Milo* is the most famous sculpture and, after the *Mona Lisa*, the most famous work of art in the world. The hordes of visitors who jam into her alcove in the Louvre museum in Paris every day are . . . proof of her popularity."[10]

Future Directions

The Louvre's collection had changed over time, growing and shrinking in response to political events. By the latter half of the twentieth century, it was of world-class quality with several priceless pieces. French officials recognized this, and strove to display the art in the best possible way. In the 1980s, another significant change was made to the architecture of the Louvre, this time to enhance the way the museum's art was exhibited.

Louvre Highlights

Pei's Pyramid

Venus de Milo

Sully Wing

Richelieu Wing

Denon Wing

Mona Lisa

The Louvre is 653,000 square feet (60,666 sq m) and has over 30,000 works of art on display. Nearly 6 million people visit the museum every year.

An International Landmark

In 1981, FRANÇOIS Mitterrand, the president of France, decided that the Louvre needed expansion, renovation, and enhancement. The museum's floor plan was chaotic for the millions of annual visitors to the Louvre. As journalist Wolf Voneckardt described:

> Some 90% of [the Louvre's] space is crammed with exhibits of paintings and sculptures, leaving only 10% for such essentials as storage and offices, to say nothing of research and restoration facilities. For years expansion has been blocked by the fact that one entire wing of the U-shape building has been occupied by the Ministry of Finance, which Mitterrand is now moving to new quarters. . . . There is no central entrance, no orientation. Anybody who decides to take a second

look at a painting may have to retrace his steps for ten or 15 minutes.[11]

Mitterrand began the Grand Louvre Project in an effort to improve the museum's display space, to create storage space, and to modernize the building overall. He set aside a budget of $1 billion to accomplish his goals and personally appointed American architect Ieoh Ming Pei to redesign the Louvre.

At first, Pei did not have a clear vision for the project. Says Pei, "When President Mitterrand approached me, I was not so sure that anything much could or should be done about the Louvre."[12] After three months of planning, Pei decided that the museum could be revamped without making any alterations to the existing architecture. Instead, Pei wanted to reorganize the existing galleries of the Louvre and to create an additional 750,000-square-foot underground level (69,677 sq m) to give the museum the space it needed. This underground level would include a grand entrance hall, restaurants, shops, theaters, storage space, and a parking area.

A Modern Addition

The entrance to the underground level would be built on the Cour Napoléon, but the form of the entrance was initially a dilemma. As Pei explained, "You [visitors to the Louvre] need to be welcomed by some kind of great space. So you've got to have something of our period. That space must have volume, it must have light and it must have a surface identification. You have to be able to look at it and say, 'Ah, this is the entrance.'"[13]

Architect Ieoh Ming Pei indicates the frame of what would become the glass pyramid in the Cour Napoléon.

To bring daylight to an underground entrance hall, Pei decided that the hall would be built of glass walls.

Pei and his team of architects tried a number of different shapes for the glass entrance hall, including cubes, domes, and pyramids. In the end, Pei chose to build the entry to the Louvre in the shape of a pyramid, modeled after the ancient Egyptian pyramid at Giza. Pei felt this form would be distinctive and unique, but would balance the Louvre's existing classic architecture.

Pei decided that the pyramid's base would be 116 feet (35.4m) square and that the structure would be 71 feet (21.6m) tall—two-thirds of the height of the Louvre's facade. At this height, the pyramid would create an impact, but would not overwhelm the view of the Louvre from nearby locations. Surrounding the pyramid entrance would be three smaller pyramids directly to the north, east, and south. These smaller pyramids would act as skylights for the underground level. All four pyramids would be made of glass and steel—materials that would complement the existing structures without duplicating or competing with them.

The Problem of Glass

Choosing the glass for Pei's pyramids was an important decision. The pyramid entrance is made of 675 diamond-shaped and 118 triangular pieces of glass. Pei felt strongly that the glass should be perfectly clear and flat in order to guarantee that the pyramid be transparent. This posed a problem—almost all of the glass made by modern manufacturers has a slightly greenish tint caused by the iron oxide used in production.

Pei learned of a century-old French glass manufacturer called Saint-Gobain that had historically made totally clear glass. This process, however, had been abandoned years before Pei's project began. Experts at Saint-Gobain insisted at first that what Pei wanted would be impossible, but eventually agreed to attempt to re-create the older process.

A New Draw for an Old Attraction

In 2003, a little-known author named Dan Brown published a novel called *The Da Vinci Code*. In it, the characters attempt to solve a centuries-old puzzle for which many of the clues are found in the Louvre. In fact, the novel opens at the Louvre, in the Grande Galerie.

Brown's novel has sold more than 25 million copies and has remained on the best-seller list since its release. In addition, enthusiasm for the book has led to increased tourism at the Louvre. The museum's tour guides now point out truths and falsehoods in Brown's descriptions of the Louvre. For example, one of the characters in the novel is a seventy-six-year-old curator. Jacque le Roux, an art historian and Louvre tour guide, explains to his tour groups that the mandatory retirement age in France is sixty-five. Also, according to CNN article, "Hunt for 'Code' Clues in France," le Roux states, "They say as well that he [the curator] closes the security system with an iron gate. . . . There is no iron gate but a wood door. It's the possibility that is fun for us to show during the tour."

The Da Vinci Code tourists, however, are not mocked by Louvre employees. Rather, they are welcomed as any other visitor. Says le Roux, "There is no bad reason to come to the Louvre."

Dan Brown's 2003 novel, The Da Vinci Code, *has drawn countless tourists to the Louvre, where much of the novel takes place.*

Saint-Gobain realized that pure white sand from a quarry at Fontainebleau could be used to produce the perfectly clear glass that Pei wanted. Though this created glass of the correct color, the glass manufacturers were forced to use a much older technique of producing glass in order to work with the new materials. The older technique produced glass panes that were not flat. Therefore, this glass would create a distorted view.

To fix the problem of the distortion, Pei sent the clear panes to the United Kingdom. There, facilities existed that could polish the Saint-Gobain glass until it was perfectly flat. The resulting panes were 0.8 inches (21mm) thick. In this way, Pei was able to achieve the effect he desired.

A Web of Support

After the glass panes were finished, Pei needed to figure out how to build the support system. Pei had envisioned a steel web to hold the glass panes. Traditional materials used by architects, however, were too bulky to fit Pei's vision. Instead, he turned to high-strength steel rods made to be used as rigging on racing sailboats. These rods were strong enough to support the heavy glass panes but thin enough to minimize obstruction of the view through the pyramid. In addition, the rigging was designed to keep from corroding over time, which made the maintenance of Pei's pyramid much easier. In the end, 128 crisscrossing steel rods secured by sixteen thin cables were used in the frame that supported the finished pyramid. Altogether, the support system and glass used in the pyramid entrance weighs more than 180 tons (163 metric tons).

The Pyramid Opens

In 1989, the pyramid entry was completed and opened to the public. More than 100,000 people attended the pyramid's grand opening. *New York Times* reporter Paul Goldberger described the opening as follows:

> The pyramid was at first bitterly denounced by many prominent people in the arts, who viewed it as an unwelcome intrusion of harsh modernism into the sacred precincts of Paris. But . . . the Parisian mood mellowed as construction proceeded. Now that the pyramid is finished, its sharpest critics seem to have retreated, and it has become fashionable in this city not only to accept the building but even to express genuine enthusiasm for it.[14]

With the opening of Pei's pyramid, the number of visitors to the Louvre grew from 2.7 million in 1988 to 4.9 million in 1992. In 2003, the number was even larger—an estimated 5.7 million people visited the Louvre. In fact, apart from the Eiffel Tower, more people buy tickets to visit the Louvre than any other landmark in France.

The renovations created a great deal of additional display space—from 336,000 square feet (31,215 sq m) in 1983 to 653,000 square feet (60,666 sq m). This allows the Louvre to exhibit more than 30,000 works of art. As a result of the centuries of additions made to the building, at present the Louvre is the longest

The modern design of the Louvre's glass pyramid stands in sharp contrast to the traditional architecture of the palace.

building in Europe. In fact, the building is longer than three Eiffel Towers laid out on their sides—the Louvre's total perimeter is more than 3 miles (4.8km).

Blending the Past, Present, and Future

The success of Mitterrand's Grand Louvre project gave the Louvre a new life. The most impressive aspect of the project, however, was that it did not attempt to create a modern museum for modern times. Instead, Mitterrand, like so many French leaders before him, insisted that the history of the Louvre be respected. The Grand Louvre Project combined with the previous eight centuries of change to create a unique and extraordinary building. The Louvre once represented the power of the French kings. Today, it represents beauty and art throughout the world. No longer a French landmark, the Louvre has become a truly global landmark.

Notes

Introduction: Centuries in the Making

1. Nicolas d'Archimbaud, *Louvre: Portrait of a Museum*. Paris: Editions Robert Laffont, 1997, p. 34.
2. Genevieve Bresc-Bautier, *The Louvre*. New York: Vendome Press, 1995, p. 202.

Chapter 1: A Royal Heritage

3. Alexandra Bonfante-Warren, *The Louvre*. Westport, CT: Hugh Lauter Levin Associates, 2000, p. 13.
4. Bresc-Bautier, *The Louvre*, p. 39.
5. Bresc-Bautier, *The Louvre*, p. 66.

Chapter 2: An Idea for a Museum

6. Quoted in d'Archimbaud, *Louvre: Portrait of a Museum*, p. 22.
7. d'Archimbaud, *Louvre: Portrait of a Museum*, p. 23.
8. Quoted in Bresc-Bautier, *The Louvre*, p. 92.

9. Quoted in d'Archimbaud, *Louvre: Portrait of a Museum*, p. 51.

Chapter 3: A World-Class Collection

10. Gregory Curtis, "Base Deception," *Smithsonian Magazine*, October 2003, www.smithsonianmag.si.edu/smithsonian/issues03/oct03/presence.html.

Chapter 4: An International Landmark

11. Wolf Voneckardt, "Pei's Pyramid Perplexes Paris," *Time Magazine*, February 27, 1984, www.time.com.
12. Quoted in Voneckardt, "Pei's Pyramid Perplexes Paris."
13. Quoted in Richard Bernstein, "I.M. Pei's Pyramid," *New York Times*, November 24, 1985, p. SM66.
14. Paul Goldberger, "Pei Pyramid and New Louvre Open Today," *New York Times*, March 29, 1989, p. C14.

Chronology

1190 Philippe Auguste builds a fortress on a site called the Louvre.

1364–1369 Raymond du Temple remodels the Louvre.

February 1528 François I demolishes the Great Tower.

1546 Pierre Lescot and Jean Goujon begin remodeling the Louvre.

1547 François I dies; work continues under Henri II.

1556 Pavilion du Roi is built.

1564 Construction begins on the Tuileries.

1566 Construction on the Petite Galerie begins.

1594 Henri de Bourbon crowned King Henri IV.

1595 Louis Métézeau and Jacques Androuet du Cerceau begin construction on the Grande Galerie; Grand Dessein is planned.

1610 Henri IV dies.

1624 Work on the Louvre begins again during Louis XIII's reign.

1660 Louis XIV begins work on the Grand Dessein.

1665 Bernini comes to Paris to design the Colonnade.

June 17, 1665 Louis XIV lays the first stone of Bernini's Colonnade.

1667 Work begins on the Colonnade, using the design put forth by Le Vau, Perrault, and LeBrun.

1674 Louis XIV leaves the Louvre to live at Versailles.

August 10, 1793 The Louvre becomes the Musée Central de la République.

1803 Musée Central de la République is renamed Musée Napoléon.

1804 Napoléon Bonaparte is crowned emperor of France.

1806–1808 Arc de Triomphe du Carrousel is built.

1851 Napoléon's nephew is crowned Emperor Napoléon III.

1852 Louis-Tullius-Joachim Visconti is appointed to design the final wing of the Louvre complex.

August 14, 1857 Construction on the Louvre begins under Hector-Martin Lefuel after Visconti's death.

May 23, 1871 Tuileries is burned down.

1882 Remains of the Tuileries demolished.

September 1981 François Mitterrand begins Grand Louvre Project.

March 30, 1989 The pyramid entry is completed and officially opened to the

Glossary

colonnade—A row of columns joined at their tops by a roof.

facade—The decorative outer layers of walls.

keep—A tower within the outer walls of a castle.

lintel—A horizontal beam of stones that runs across the top of a row of columns.

oculi—Large circular windows.

pediment—A triangular structure that tops a building.

polychromy—The use of different materials to create a multicolored effect.

quoin—The blocks which line the vertical sides of a facade.

relief—Decorative scenes carved onto flat stone surfaces.

vermiculated rustication—A pattern carved into stone to look like worms have burrowed into the surface.

For More Information

Books

Nicolas d'Archimbaud, *Louvre: Portrait of a Museum*. Paris: Editions Robert Laffont, 1997.

Emile Biasini, Jean Lebrat, Dominique Bezombes, and Jean-Michel Vincent, *The Grand Louvre: A Museum Transfigured 1981–1993*. New York: Nichols, 1990.

Michael Laclotte, *Treasures of the Louvre*. New York: Abbeville Press, 1993.

Periodicals

Richard Bernstein, "I.M. Pei's Pyramid," *New York Times*, November 24, 1985, p. SM66.

Gregory Curtis, "Base Deception," *Smithsonian Magazine*, October 2003, www.smithsonian mag.si.edu/smithsonian/issues03/oct03/presence.html.

Paul Goldberger, "Pei Pyramid and New Louvre Open Today," *New York Times*, March 29, 1989, p. C14.

Anne Rochette and Wade Saunders, "Revitalizing the Louvre," *Art in America*, June 1994, www.findarticles.com/p/articles/mi_m1248/is_n6_v82/ai_15490854.

Wolf Voneckardt, "Pei's Pyramid Perplexes Paris," *Time Magazine*, February 27, 1984, www.time.com.

Web Sites

The Louvre, The Paris Pages (www.paris.org/Musees/Louvre). Includes information about the Louvre's collections and the history of the museum and the building.

The Official Site of the Louvre (www.louvre.fr). Contains a wealth of information about the Louvre, in terms of both its history and its art collections, as well as a virtual tour of the museum.

Index